SO YOU'RE A
GRAND PARENT!

Mike Haskins & Clive Whichelow
Illustrations by Ian Baker

summersdale

SO YOU'RE A GRANDPARENT!

First published in 2008

This edition copyright © Mike Haskins and Clive Whichelow, 2017

Illustrations by Ian Baker

Summersdale Publishers Ltd
46 West Street
Chichester
West Sussex
PO19 1RP
UK

www.summersdale.com

Printed and bound in China

ISBN: 978-1-78685-047-8

Substantial discounts on bulk quantities of Summersdale books are available to corporations, professional associations and other organisations. For details contact general enquiries: telephone: +44 (0) 1243 771107, fax: +44 (0) 1243 786300 or email: enquiries@summersdale.com.

INTRODUCTION

Hello Grandad/Grandma!

Oh no! There's a name you never thought you'd have!

Not when you're still such a lithe desirable sexy young thing (even if you do say so yourself). Not someone still in the prime of life (this is still you we're talking about by the way), someone who still wears jeans, listens to loud music and, if not in mint condition, is still in reasonably full working order.

Nevertheless, your name has now officially been changed.

And it's not just going to be the grandchildren who call you that, is it? From now on that's the way their mum and dad are going to refer to you all the time too. It's going to make people think that you're their grandparents as well!

However old you really are and whatever you may actually look like, your new name will conjure up images of grey hair, walking sticks and dreadful soup-stained old cardigans. And to your grandchildren you'll seem as though you're from another century. Come to think of it, you are from another century. Scary or what?

But that's not the worst thing. Oh no! Cast your mind back to when your kids were little. Remember when they kept pleading with you to buy them a puppy, a kitten, a rabbit, or any kind of little pet?

'Oh no!' you told them. 'Because I'll tell you exactly what will happen. Pretty soon you'll find you're far too busy and I'll be the one who ends up looking after them each day and cleaning up all the mess.'

Isn't that exactly what has just happened now? Except this time you don't have a receipt to take back to the pet shop for a refund?

Never mind, your grandchildren are absolutely lovely, aren't they?

Just look at them!

OK, better fetch some disinfectant and a cleaning cloth quickly and then you can consider how lovely they are.

THE BASIC MYTHS ABOUT BEING A GRANDPARENT

Your grandchildren will regard you as a wonderful, twinkly-eyed old character – more likely your grandchildren will constantly tell you that you smell funny.

It's all the pleasure and none of the problems of being a parent – no, it's all the pleasure and none of the child benefit payments!

Being with your grandchildren will give you a new lease of life – if they don't cause your premature demise first.

THE ADVANTAGES OF BEING A GRANDPARENT

You can smugly talk about how much
harder it was bringing up babies
in your day – your kids were too
young back then to remember.

You can bribe the kids by offering them
all the things their mum and dad say
they must definitely never have.

If the kids play up when
you're out with them you can tell
passers-by it's all the parents' fault.

The kids can act as your spies to keep you informed about what's really going on between their mum and dad.

THE DRAWBACKS OF BEING A GRANDPARENT

Your redundancy pay-off
will be severely dented by
trips to theme parks.

You're now officially a free
babysitting service.

Half the kids' toys in the attic
you wanted to pass on are now
deemed politically incorrect.

When you try to help your
grandchildren with their homework
you're told, 'We don't do it
that way any more.'

ESSENTIAL REQUIREMENTS FOR BEING A GRANDAD

The magical ability to
produce coins from behind
children's ears

A selection of elderly, yellowing
board games which you insist
are more fun than an afternoon
messing about on an iPad

A big bald head shiny
enough for the grandchildren
to see their reflections in

Physical oddities such as
big ears or a hairy nose that
can be gleefully pointed out to
everyone at family gatherings

A war wound or at least something that could conceivably pass for one, e.g. a particularly deep wrinkle

ESSENTIAL REQUIREMENTS FOR BEING A GRANDMA

A degree of patience that
passeth all understanding

A variety of fail-safe recipes for
cakes, biscuits, buns, etc.

Photograph albums of the children's parents when they were small – particularly appealing when they were screaming their heads off over something

An old tin full of buttons that are strangely more fascinating than any toy ever invented

A giant dressing-up box of bizarre and comical outfits (i.e. your wardrobe)

DIFFERENT WAYS YOU WILL BE ASKED: 'ARE YOU AVAILABLE FOR BABYSITTING?'

'The kids keep asking when they can see Grandma and Grandad again.'

'It must get a bit dull for you sitting in your house night after night...'

'Do you know, the kids absolutely love
having you tell them a bedtime story.'

'Trust me, they're all tucked up in bed
and fast asleep each night by 6.30 p.m.'

THINGS YOU WILL COME TO KNOW A LOT ABOUT

The lifestyles, thoughts and opinions of the entire population of the Isle of Struay

All the latest playground insults

The words (if you can call them words) to all the latest pop songs (if you can call them songs)

Details of the goriest horror films currently available on Netflix

The names of all
the up-and-coming
gangsta rappers

DISCIPLINING CHILDREN THE GRANDPARENT WAY

'If you don't behave I will take
my teeth out in front of you.'

'If you don't behave, your dinner
will be whatever I can find in
my kitchen cupboard that's
furthest past its use-by date.'

'Don't forget that because I am so old
I know a lot of people who have died
and if necessary I will contact them and
get them to come and haunt you.'

'There'll be no rides for you when
I get my stairlift and mobility
scooter in a few years' time!'

THINGS YOU'D FORGOTTEN ABOUT SMALL CHILDREN

The surprising amount
they actually weigh

They have no inhibitions
about pointing out the most
personal and embarrassing of
things in the loudest of voices

They don't enjoy looking round old churches or having a 'nice sit down'

They view every one of your possessions as a new toy

GRANDPARENT BEHAVIOUR YOU WILL FIND YOURSELF FALLING INTO

Recounting details of
your childhood as though
it was spent in Dickensian
squalor and poverty

Pretending to be a little bit deafer, more fragile, more forgetful, etc. than you actually are

Threatening to tell a policeman/ Father Christmas/the Tooth Fairy about bad behaviour

TELLTALE SIGNS THAT YOU'RE A GRANDPARENT

'Baby on board' sticker on
your stairlift

Crayon 'artwork' on
your fridge door

What looks like the local police station's entire fingerprint collection over your walls and furniture

Misshapen plastic safety covers over your plug sockets covered in teeth marks

PRESENTS YOU WILL BE GIVEN BY YOUR GRANDCHILDREN

Near replicas of heirlooms which have recently met with unfortunate accidents

Various pieces of jewellery made from dried pasta, feathers, seashells, etc.

A painting of what would appear
to be the oldest person ever
to have lived with your name
scrawled across the bottom

A clay model of an animal that cannot quite be identified

A box of chocolates which they will immediately insist on unwrapping and helping you to eat

THE GRANDPARENT'S DAILY SCHEDULE

7.00 a.m. Get up

7.10 a.m. Make nice cup of tea

7.25 a.m. Babysitting hotline rings

7.26 a.m. Listen to apologies and excuses prefacing request for you to babysit yet again

7.45 a.m. Ring on doorbell

8.00 a.m. The next few hours pass in something of a blur

7.00 p.m.-ish Parents collect kids, apologise for lateness, say they hope the kids haven't been too much trouble

7.15 p.m. Five minutes restoring the house to something like order before the next blitzkrieg

8.00 p.m. Another nice cup of tea

8.15 p.m. Pass out exhausted

HOW YOUR GRANDCHILDREN WILL PERCEIVE YOU

As an ultimate authority and source of wisdom on all matters (apart from new technology)

As virtually indestructible

As 'option B' when their parents refuse them something

As a strange wrinkled being with an extremely tidy house

As the only person in the world who can tell *their* mum and dad off

That person who stands there waving with a stupid grin on their face every single time you go past them on the merry-go-round

WHITE LIES TOLD BY GRANDPARENTS

'Grandad/Grandma has a very weak
heart so it's important for you to be
very quiet and well-behaved…'

'I most certainly do have Father
Christmas' mobile phone number.'

'I'm not allowed in theme
parks at my age.'

'Well, they certainly didn't learn
that kind of language from me.'

THINGS YOU WILL NOW FIND AROUND YOUR HOUSE

Various artefacts inscribed with the legend, 'To the best grandad/ grandma in the world'

A range of toys that came as free gifts with kiddies' burger meals

Leaflets for all tourist attractions
within a 20-mile radius

Half-chewed sweets, biscuits and sticky things that aren't even meant to be sticky

Strange wet patches

PHRASES YOU'LL NOW FIND YOURSELF USING

'Five hundred pounds for a pram? We've still got your old one in the attic.'

'If I'd said that to my father he would have knocked me into the middle of next week.'

'They don't know
they're born do they?'

And remember, even if you've
only got one grandchild at the
moment, call them 'dear' – it'll save
remembering all those names when
the rest of the brood arrives.

PHRASES YOU REALLY SHOULDN'T USE NOW YOU'RE A GRANDPARENT

'Five pounds for a new
dummy? We've still got your
old one in the attic.'

'Dig my allotment and
this entire shiny five-pence
piece can be yours.'

'It's funny, you don't look a
bit like your father...'

'Oh get up there! I always
had to clean the chimney
when I was your age!'

THINGS YOUR GRANDCHILDREN WILL TEACH YOU

How to work your iPad, DVD
player and mobile phone

That there are very good
reasons why you are biologically
prevented from having children
after a certain age

That you are destroying
the planet and personally
murdering all the polar bears

BARGAINING COUNTERS THAT YOU CAN USE AS A GRANDPARENT

'If you pay for satellite TV for us the kids can watch cartoons when they come over.'

'Of course we wouldn't be
able to do all this babysitting
if you put us in a home.'

'The kids said next time you bring
them round they'll show us how
to put some of those old photos
of you up on the internet...'

BAD WAYS GRANDPARENTS CAN ENTERTAIN THE GRANDCHILDREN

Performing ill-advised attempts
at contortionism

Letting them do exactly what
they say they want to do

Taking out false teeth
and gurning

BAD WAYS GRANDCHILDREN CAN ENTERTAIN GRANDPARENTS

Making an impromptu piece of modern art involving granny's sofa and a tub of nappy rash cream

Testing out their new teeth on legs (human or furniture)

Hiding and/or sampling
grandad or grandma's various
prescription medicines

Acting out an aerial stunt
sequence they recently saw
in a superhero movie

THINGS PEOPLE WILL NOW SAY TO YOU

'You look far too young to be a grandparent.' (You wish!)

'Oh they'll give you a new lease of life!' (You poor old codger.)

'They're quite a handful aren't they?' (This phrase usually prefaces the speaker making his or her excuses and leaving you to it.)

'It must really bring back what it was like when your own children were little.' (Yes it does and that's why we didn't have any more of them.)

'Nan Nan' or 'Dag Dag' (This is your new long-lost Teletubby name which your grandchildren will call you extremely loudly in public places.)

MAIN EVENTS YOU CAN LOOK FORWARD TO

Seeing them take their first
faltering steps

Hearing them say their
first words

Their first solid foods

Becoming a great-grandparent

Those first little teeth
coming through

EVENTS IT'S LESS EASY TO LOOK FORWARD TO

Their first solid foods coming
back in slightly less solid form

Them growing up and wanting
£100 trainers for Christmas

Hearing them say their first
swear words

YOUR NEW
SOCIAL CIRCLE

Small friends of your
grandchildren

The owner of your local
sweet shop

The occasional
head louse

GRANDPARENTS' CV

Skills: getting to the end of one's tether and having to find a just a little bit more tether, seeing the good in children when no one else can

Education: school of hard knocks, university of life, night school of sleep deprivation

Qualifications: Oh! Levels in children's shocking behaviour, Ah! Levels in indulgence

WORDS OF WISDOM YOUR GRANDCHILDREN WILL SHARE WITH YOU

'Mummy/Daddy says you've lost your marbles. Shall I help you find them?'

'Are your ears and nose getting bigger or are they staying the same size while the rest of your head shrinks?'

'Grandma has lots of
lines on her face.'

THINGS YOU REALLY SHOULDN'T BUY FOR YOUR GRANDCHILDREN

Toys that require £10 worth of batteries every three days

Any toy that genuinely fires, shoots, hammers, drills or makes food that they will seriously expect you to sample

Any toy that you will end up having to construct

ADVICE YOU WISH YOU'D BEEN GIVEN

If you have lots of children you will have twice as many grandchildren

Get all babysitting arrangements in writing

Don't give them food that can:
a) be broken into tiny pieces,
b) smeared or c) stain

If you're interested in finding out
more about our books, find us on
Facebook at **Summersdale Publishers**
and follow us on Twitter
at **@Summersdale**.

www.summersdale.com